ILLUSTRATED CLASSIC EDITIONS

David Copperfield

Charles Dickens

3019

**Illustrations by
Pablo Marcos Studio**

BARONET BOOKS, New York, New York

ILLUSTRATED CLASSIC EDITIONS

edited by
Malvina G. Vogel

Contents

About the Author

Charles Dickens was born in 1812 in Landport, Portsea, England. He was the second child of eight in a family that moved frequently because of money problems. When Charles was twelve, his father was thrown into debtor's prison. The boy left school for a while and went to work in a warehouse.

At twenty, Dickens became a newspaperman and reported law cases and Parliamentary debates. He also began writing short stories for magazines, signing them "Boz," his youngest brother's nickname. Dickens was soon a well-known reformer as well as

Dancing in the Parlor

David Reads to Peggotty.

CHAPTER 2

A Change in My Life

When I was eight years old, Peggotty and I were sitting one night by the parlor fire, alone. I had been reading to her about crocodiles. Perhaps I wasn't reading very well, for after I was finished, Peggotty had the impression that crocodiles, or "crorkindills," as she called them, were some sort of vegetable.

After we read a while, my mother came in with a gentleman who had walked home with us from church Sunday.

Mr. Murdstone—I knew him by that name now—visited us often. I didn't like him or his deep voice. And I remember Peggotty getting a strange look on her face when he appeared. It seemed the next day, but it was probably about two months afterwards that Peggotty said coaxingly, "Master Davy, how should you like to go along with me and spend a fortnight at my brother's house at Yarmouth? There's the sea and the boats and the fishermen and the beach and my nephew, Ham."

"That would be a treat," I replied, "but I don't want to leave Mama alone."

"Your mama's going off on a visit elsewhere," said Peggotty, and again I saw that strange look come over her face.

As our cart pulled away from the house heading towards the road to Yarmouth, Mr. Murdstone came up to where my mother was standing, waving good-bye. I wondered what business it was of his being there.

The cart driver, Mr. Barkis, was a friendly man, and he and Peggotty laughed a lot during the long trip.

When we reached the streets of Yarmouth,

Leaving for Yarmouth

DAVID COPPERFIELD

I smelled the fish and pitch and tar and salt air. I saw sailors walking about and carts jingling along the stone streets.

Ham met us in the town. He was a huge, strong fellow, six feet tall, but with a boyish face. Ham carried me on his back and a small box of ours under his arm. With Peggotty carrying another box, we went past gas works, boatyards, blacksmiths' forges, and riggers' lofts until we came to a flat stretch of land along the sea.

"Yon's our house, Mas'r Davy!" said Ham.

I looked in all directions—as far as I could stare over the land and away at the sea and away at the river. But I saw no house.

The only thing in view was a black barge, or some kind of outdated boat, high and dry on the ground. Windows and a door were cut into it, and an iron funnel stuck out of it like a chimney, smoking very cozily. Nothing else like a house was visible to *me:*

"That ship-looking thing?" I asked.

"Yon's Our House."

"That's it, Mas'r Davy," replied Ham.

If it had been Aladdin's palace, I could not have been more enchanted with the idea of living in it.

Peggotty opened a little door in the stern of the barge and showed me my bedroom. There was a little window where the rudder used to go through, a mirror just the right height for me, a little bed with just enough room to get into it, and a tiny bouquet of seaweed in a blue mug on the table.

We were welcomed by a very courteous woman in a white apron and by a beautiful little girl with blue eyes and long yellow curls.

Peggotty explained, "This is Mrs. Gummidge, a widow lady who keeps house for Mr. Peggotty."

I smiled at the old woman.

"And that little girl," Peggotty went on, "is Emily. She is my brother's adopted niece. You see, Master Davy, she is an orphan, just

David Meets Emily.

like Ham. And my good brother, good as gold Mr. Peggotty is, adopted both Emily and Ham at different times."

After a while, Mr. Peggotty came in, and I saw that he was a good-natured man, just as Peggotty had said.

Almost as soon as morning shone upon the oyster-shell frame of my mirror, I was out of bed and out with little Emily, picking up stones upon the beach.

I told Emily all about my mother and how we only had each other and how I was going to grow up right away and take care of her.

Emily told me how she wanted to be a fine lady when she grew up. She had lost her mother, and her father drowned at sea.

We spent most of my fortnight together, playing on the beach, going out on Ham's boat, and talking. Before my visit was over, I was quite in love with little Emily.

All the time I had been on my visit, I had thought very little of home. But the fortnight

Picking Up Stones on the Beach

flew by, and soon it was time to leave. After tearful farewells, we left Yarmouth. The closer to home we came, the more excited I got to be going there. But Peggotty was out of sorts during the trip back. The strange look was on her face again.

My mother wasn't at the door to greet us, and I was frightened when Peggotty took my hand and led me into the kitchen.

"Where's Mama?" I cried. "She's not *dead* like my father, is she?"

"No, no, Master Davy," she said. "Your mama's not dead. She's married. You've got a new pa. Come and see him."

"I don't want to see him," I shouted.

But Peggotty insisted and since I wanted to see my mother, I followed her into the parlor. I found my mother sitting near the fire, and there beside her was—Mr. Murdstone. He warned my mother to control herself, so she came to me slowly and timidly, and kissed me. I shook hands with Mr. Murdstone, but

A New Father

as soon as I could get away, I crept upstairs.

But my bedroom had been changed. I was now to sleep far away from my mother.

From that time on, I hated and feared Mr. Murdstone. My mother held me hurriedly, only when he was not near. With this change in the house, it no longer felt like my home. Mr. Murdstone meant to reform our lives with his firmness, but I could not respect him or even like him. My only comfort was in the kitchen with Peggotty.

Then, to make things even worse, Mr. Murdstone's elder sister, Miss Jane Murdstone, came to live with us. She made it very clear that she didn't like me, and I soon began spending my days in my own little bedroom, reading some old books that once belonged to my dead father.

Mr. Murdstone and his sister talked of sending me to boarding school, but until they decided, I continued learning my lessons at home from my mother. I recited them to her,

David Learns His Lessons.

but that man and his sister were always present, so that everything I ever studied left my head, and I stuttered and stumbled.

Mr. Murdstone said I needed more discipline, and one day he took me to my room to teach me obedience. When we got there, he suddenly threw me across his lap.

"Mr. Murdstone! Sir!" I cried. "Don't! Pray don't beat me! I have tried to learn, sir, but I can't learn while you and Miss Murdstone are watching. I can't!"

"Can't you, David? We'll see," he said. And he hit me heavily with his cane.

I cried out in pain and begged him not to beat me. But the blows fell again and again. Then I suddenly grabbed his hand and bit it.

He beat me then as if he were trying to beat me to death. I heard my mother and Peggotty crying out to him from outside the door. Then he was gone, and my door was locked from the outside.

I was kept a prisoner in my room for five

I Was Locked in My Room.

DAVID COPPERFIELD

days. I was not even allowed to see my mother. The last night, as I watched the rain coming down faster and faster between me and the church, Peggotty came to my door. Through the keyhole, she whispered, "Master Davy, you are to be sent away to school near London. But do not worry. I will take care of your mother." Then before she left, she kissed the keyhole, for she couldn't kiss me.

In the morning when I was let out of my room, I saw my mother. She was pale, and her eyes were red. Mr. Murdstone would not even let her hug me when I left.

Mr. Barkis loaded my things into his cart, and we were off. We had gone only half a mile along the road when Peggotty burst out of the bushes and climbed in. She said nothing, but hugged me and gave me some cakes, three shillings, two half-crowns, and a note from my mother. Then she was gone.

During the ride Mr. Barkis asked me many questions about Peggotty. He seemed most

Peggotty Whispers Through the Keyhole.

interested when I told him Peggotty wasn't married, and he told me that when I wrote to her, I was to tell her that "Barkis is willin'." I was puzzled at the time by the message, but I later learned that Barkis wanted to marry my good Peggotty, but was too shy to ask.

London was too far for Barkis to go, so I had to take another coach, a night coach, to London. But when I reached the coach station, there was no one to meet a child called Copperfield or Murdstone. I stood wondering how long it would take me to walk back home when a thin young man stepped up to me and asked, "You're the new boy?"

This was Mr. Mell, one of the masters at Salem House, the school I was to attend.

Salem House was empty when we arrived. I had been sent to the school at holiday time as a punishment. My teeth were to be filed down to prevent further biting, but even worse, I was made to wear a sign that read: WATCH OUT FOR HIM. HE BITES.

No One To Meet David

Mr. Creakle, the Headmaster

CHAPTER 3

My "First Half" at Salem House

I had lessons with Mr. Mell for a month and was doing well when I was fetched to appear before Mr. Creakle, the headmaster.

Mr. Creakle's face was fiery and his eyes were small. He had a little nose, a large chin, and was bald on top of his head.

"So! This is the young gentleman who needs to be taught obedience, who needs to have his teeth filed so he won't bite. I have the happiness of knowing your stepfather," said Mr. Creakle, taking me by the ear. "He is a good man."

Mr. Creakle was no gentler than Mr.

Murdstone, and I was very glad to be ordered out of his office.

The first boy who returned to school introduced himself as Tommy Traddles. He enjoyed my sign so much that he saved me embarrassment by making a joke of it for the other boys.

Then I was introduced to James Steerforth. He was about six years my senior then, very good-looking, and an excellent student. He explained that it was proper for a new boy to treat the others to a secret feast and offered to buy a bottle of currant wine, biscuits, and some fruit and smuggle it into my room.

I agreed, even though it meant spending the last half-crown my mother had given me.

That night, he laid the feast out on my bed. The other boys in the room joined us, grouped on the nearest beds or on the floor. How well I remember our sitting there, talking in whispers. The boys told me stories about the school and the masters.

A Secret Feast

After many hours of such talk, we went to bed. And from that night on, big handsome Steerforth took me under his protection.

I thought of him for a long time after I went to bed and finally sat up to look at him. He lay with his face turned up and his head resting easily on his arm. I would come to know that as his favorite position.

School began in earnest next day. The schoolroom became hushed as death when Mr. Creakle entered. He walked over to me and said, "So, young man, I hear you are famous for biting. Well, I am famous for biting too." He proved it by beating me and most of the other boys that day. Because my sign was in the way of his cane, it was soon taken off.

Poor Traddles, I think he was caned every day that half-year so were all the other boys ... all, that is, except James Steerforth.

One day I told Steerforth about the stories I had read from my father's library.

A Schoolroom Hushed As Death

"And do you remember them?" he asked.

"Oh yes," I replied. "I have a good memory."

"I tell you what, young Copperfield," he said. "I can't sleep well, so you shall tell 'em to me. We'll go over 'em one after another and make a regular Arabian Nights of it."

That night we began. I lay in my bed, telling the stories in the dark, changing my voice for the different characters. Traddles was a sort of chorus, adding sound effects.

In return for this, Steerforth helped me with my arithmetic and kept the other boys from tormenting me.

Even though Salem House was not noted for its high scholarship, I did make good progress because I was a good reader and was enjoying my first chance at a real education.

The holidays were coming. The counting of weeks became days. I was afraid that Mr. Murdstone would not send for me, but one day Steerforth brought me a letter from my mother saying that I was to go home.

Stories with Traddles' Sound Effects

Overjoyed at a New Baby Brother!

CHAPTER 4

My Mother Dies

Mr. Barkis, the carriage driver, greeted me at the coach station as if not five minutes had passed since last we met. He asked me about Peggotty, and I told him that I had delivered his "Barkis is willin'" message.

He left me at the garden gate. I feared at every step to see the faces of Mr. or Miss Murdstone glaring at me from a window. But much to my joy, they were not there. As I neared the door, I heard my mother singing in the parlor, and I went softly into the room. She was sitting by the fire feeding an infant, my new baby brother. I was overjoyed!

Mr. and Miss Murdstone were out for the evening, so Mother and Peggotty and I dined together by the fireside. I gave Peggotty the message from Barkis again. She covered her face with her apron and laughed.

"Oh, drat the man!" cried Peggotty. "He wants to marry me. But I wouldn't have him or anybody!"

"But, Peggotty dear," said my mother gently, "you should marry some day. But don't leave me now."

"I'll not leave till I'm too deaf and too lame and too blind, and then I'll go to my Davy and ask him to take me in."

"And I shall welcome you as a queen," I said to my dear nurse.

Later, we sat around the fire. My mother held me in her arms the way she used to, then when my little baby brother was awake, I took him in my arms.

As we sat talking about family and friends, Peggotty asked a question from out of

David Takes His Brother in His Arms.

nowhere. "What's become of Davy's great-aunt?"

"Best to leave Aunt Betsey in her cottage by the sea," said my mother, "unless you want another visit from her."

"Lord forbid!" cried Peggotty. "But I wonder if she's forgiven Davy for being a boy."

That night was the only happy time of my month's vacation, because the next day, Miss Murdstone put an end to my dining with Peggotty and to my holding my brother.

I was not sorry to go. But when I left my mother at the garden gate, I felt sad.

Two months later I was called out of class and into the parlor at Salem House. It was my tenth birthday, and I expected that it was a package from Peggotty. I found Mrs. Creakle, the headmaster's wife, with a letter in her hand. She looked at me gravely and said, "I'm sorry, David, but your mother and brother have died."

"Your Mother and Brother Have Died."

Mrs. Creakle kept me in the parlor all day. I cried and slept, then awoke and cried again. The next day I said good-bye to Traddles and Steerforth, little realizing that I would never return to school again.

When I reached home, I was in Peggotty's arms before I reached the door. She looked tired and drawn, for she had sat up day and night with my mother during her last days.

I was fitted for a black suit for the funeral. As I stood crying at my mother's grave, I felt more lost and more lonely than ever before in my ten years of life.

With my mother gone, the first thing Miss Murdstone did after the funeral was to dismiss Peggotty. As to me or my future, not a word was said. I think they would have been happy if they could dismiss me with a month's notice too. Finally, I was told that I was not going back to school at all.

Mr. and Miss Murdstone payed no attention to me. Peggotty could find no work

The Funeral

nearby and planned to go to live with her brother at Yarmouth. More than anything, I wanted to go with her and tell little Emily of my troubles. When I asked about going, Miss Murdstone seemed very agreeable to the thought of getting me out of the house. So I left with Peggotty.

All the way to Yarmouth Mr. Barkis grinned at Peggotty.

The days by the sea passed much as they had before. I told my friends about school, about Steerforth and Traddles. Nothing was said about my mother's death. Everyone was especially kind to me.

One day, Peggotty and Barkis took Emily and me for a ride in the cart. They stopped the cart in front of the church, and Peggotty and Barkis went inside for a good while. When they came out, they told us they were married.

Before Peggotty went off to live in Barkis' neat cottage, she said to me, "Master Davy,

Peggotty and Barkis Are Married.

from this day on, there will be a special room in my house for you. And your crocodile book will be on the table waiting to be read whether you come tomorrow or years and years from now."

I thanked my old nurse with all my heart.

The visit ended, and I had to go home, although I hardly called it home. Day after day, week after week, I was coldly neglected. I had no mother and no Peggotty. I hoped desperately to be allowed to return to school, but that was not to be. Mr. Murdstone said he could not afford it.

Finally he decided to send me to London— to work! I was to go to a warehouse he owned with a friend of his. There, I would earn seven shillings, or $1.68, a week. With that, I would feed and clothe myself, and he would pay for my lodgings with a family who lived near the warehouse.

So there I was, ten years old, and on my way to London to work.

David Is Coldly Neglected.

Working in the Warehouse

CHAPTER 5

Life on My Own

Murdstone and Grinby's warehouse was at the water side, the last building at the bottom of a narrow street, curving downhill to the river. It was a decaying old house, overrun with rats and filled with the dirt of a hundred years. On my first morning I met some of the other boys who I was to work with. We washed and rinsed wine bottles, rejected damaged ones, pasted labels, fitted corks, and packed the finished bottles in casks.

At half-past twelve, Mr. Grinby beckoned to me to come into his office. I went in and saw a stoutish, middle-aged person with no more hair on his head than on an egg.

"This is Mr. Micawber," said Mr. Grinby.

"Ahem!" said the stranger. "That is my name. And you are David Copperfield, the boy who is to live in my house." Speaking with a flourish that outdid his shabby dress, Mr. Micawber added that he would come for me that evening to teach me the quickest route from the warehouse to his house.

He appeared on time. I washed my hands and face, and we walked to the house. It was shabby like himself. The first floor was unfurnished, and the blinds were kept down to fool the neighbors and to deceive creditors into thinking no one was at home. He presented me to Mrs. Micawber, a thin, faded lady, and their four tiny children.

Still, even though I lived here and the Micawbers tried to be kind, I had no one on earth to go to for friendship or advice. I was a frightened little stranger in a large, terrifying city. I worked from morning till night,

Mr. Micawber's Shabby House

feeling utterly miserable and without hope, and fearing that everything I had learned at school would leave me. My tears often mixed with the water as I washed the wine bottles, but I was careful never to let the other boys see me cry.

The Micawbers were kind to me, and even though they were always short of money, they often invited me to share their own hot dinner and sit with them around the fire on cold nights. The Micawbers owed many bills, and creditors came to visit them at all hours—some, quite ferocious. The Micawbers' only solution was to begin pawning their few pieces of furniture. So after work I would take a small table or a few chairs or a rug or blankets to a pawnshop and bring back a few shillings. But no matter how bad things were, Mr. Micawber would always say, "Something must turn up."

At last, Mr. Micawber's difficulties came to a crisis. He was arrested early one morning

At the Pawnshop

and taken to King's Bench Prison until he could pay his debts. His family was permitted to live with him there.

Mrs. Micawber feared for me—a 10-year-old all alone in the streets, poorly clothed and half-starved. So she found me a cheap room near enough to the prison so that I could visit them in the evenings after work.

Finally, the "something" that Mr. Micawber had been waiting for did turn up. A rich relative died in Australia and left him some money. He planned to pay off his debts and take his family there to live.

I didn't want to stay in London without them, and I suddenly remembered the stories my mother and Peggotty had told me about my eccentric aunt who had hit the doctor with her bonnet on the day of my birth because I had been born a boy. Since she was the only real relative I had in the world, I decided to find her and ask her to take me into her home. But I didn't know where she

David Visits the Micawbers in Jail.

lived, so I wrote a letter to Peggotty and asked her where Miss Betsey lived.

Peggotty's answer soon arrived, along with a half-guinea to get me to Dover where Miss Betsey lived. I planned to use it to hire a cart to take me and my small box of clothes there. But the man I hired drove off with my half-guinea and my box.

I ran after him as fast as I could. But I was left panting and crying in the mud, with only my week's pay of five shillings to get me to Dover. This was not enough to pay my fare, so I set off on foot and slept out under haystacks or in the fields at night.

At the end of six days, my money was all gone. I was hungry, thirsty, and worn-out. My shoes no longer looked like shoes. My hair hadn't seen a comb since I left London. What few clothes I had on my back were in rags, for I had pawned all the rest.

When I stumbled exhausted into Dover, I was directed by a carriage driver to Miss Betsey

Chasing a Thief

Trotwood's house. It was a neat little cottage on a cliff overlooking the sea.

I was such a miserable sight that I was afraid to knock at the door. So I stood at the gate until I saw a tall, slim, gray-haired lady come out the door. She was carrying gardeners' gloves and a pruning knife.

"Go away!" she cried when she spotted me. "No boys are allowed here!" And she marched into the garden and stopped to dig a root.

"If you please, Aunt Betsey," I said, walking up to her, trembling with fear, "I am your nephew, David Copperfield."

"Oh, Lord!" she cried and sat flat down on the garden path.

"I used to hear my dear mother speak of you before she died," I explained. "I have been neglected and mistreated since then, so I ran away and came to you. I have been walking for days and days without a bed to sleep in and...." But at that moment all the desperation of the past week broke loose, and

"Oh, Lord!"

I began to cry hysterically.

Miss Betsey got up in a great hurry and led me into the house. She put me on the sofa with a shawl under my head and brought me something to drink. Then she called out, "Mr. Dick, please come in here. I need your advice."

A pleasant-faced gentleman soon entered the room. He had a friendly smile, but his eyes held a strange faraway brightness. He seemed to have childish ways about him.

"Mr. Dick, I want some very sound advice," said Miss Betsey. "Here is young David Copperfield, the son of my late nephew. He has run away. What shall I do with him?"

"Why, I should . . . wash him," said Mr. Dick briskly, "and then feed him."

When I had bathed, they put me in a shirt and trousers of Mr. Dick's and tied me up in two or three shawls. I don't know what sort of bundle I looked like, but I felt like a very hot one. I lay on the sofa and soon fell asleep.

"Wash Him and Then Feed Him."

DAVID COPPERFIELD

When I awoke hours later, I told my aunt the story of my mother's unfortunate marriage to Mr. Murdstone and of the way he had treated me.

"Oh that murderer!" cried my aunt.

Next day, my aunt told me she had written to Mr. Murdstone, or *Mr. Murder,* as she called him.

"Does he know where I am?" I asked, alarmed.

"I have told him," she replied.

"Shall I have to go back to him?"

"I don't know. We shall see," she said, and that was all she would say about it.

After Miss Betsey saw to it that I had a good breakfast, she turned to me and said, "I would like you to go upstairs and say good morning to Mr. Dick. He's got a longer name—Richard Babley, but don't you call him by it, whatever you do. He can't bear his name. So take care, child, don't call him anything but Mr. Dick."

"Say Good Morning to Mr. Dick."

I went upstairs and found Mr. Dick working on his book—a Memorial to some Lord. He had been writing it for ten years. But he was never able to write too long without describing the beheading of King Charles every few pages. This, my aunt later explained, was a symptom of his harmless illness.

"Ha!" he cried, laying down his pen. "How does the world go? It's a mad world, boy." He laughed then—a strange laugh. Then he showed me his kite. It must have been seven feet high!

"What do you think of that for a kite?" he asked proudly.

"It's a beautiful one," I answered.

"I made it," said Mr. Dick. "We'll go and fly it, you and I."

But we did not get to fly the kite that day for I had no clothes I could move around in.

When I came back down, I asked my aunt, "Is Mr. Dick . . . out of his mind?"

"No, indeed!" cried Miss Betsey. "Mr. Dick

A Seven-Foot-High Kite!

is a distant relation of mine. He has been *called* mad by his family, and his brother had wanted to shut him up in an asylum for life. But I believed him sane and took him to live with me. That was ten years ago. He has been my best friend and adviser ever since."

For the next few days, my aunt and Mr. Dick were very kind to me. We spent many happy hours together, and I almost forgot my past. Then I would remember that my aunt had asked Mr. and Miss Murdstone to come to see her, and I would become terrified!

One morning, I saw the two of them coming up the garden path. I wanted to run and hide, but Aunt Betsey cried, "Certainly not!" So I stood off in a corner while they spoke.

"I must tell you, Miss Trotwood," began Mr. Murdstone, "that David has given us great trouble and pain. He is stubborn and has a violent temper."

"Yes," agreed Miss Murdstone, "he is the worst boy in the world."

The Murdstones Arrive.

"And we are here to take him back," added Mr. Murdstone. "I shall deal with him in the manner I think best."

"Rubbish!" cried Miss Betsey. "I don't believe a word of it. You two are no better than murderers. Your cruelty caused David's mother's death. *You* deserve to be punished for sending a ten-year-old boy out to earn his own living while you lived comfortably in a house that really belongs to David, now that his mother is dead. But I shall let David decide what he wants to do." Then turning to me, Miss Betsey asked, "Do you wish to return with them?"

"Please, Aunt Betsey," I pleaded, "don't make me go. Neither of them has ever liked me or been kind to me. They made my mama unhappy and Peggotty too. They made *me* miserable. Please don't make me go back with them."

Mr. Murdstone turned pale. Then, pointing a finger angrily at my aunt, he said, "I am

"Do You Wish To Return with Them?"

here for the first and last time to either take David and deal with him as I see fit, or to leave him with you. If he stays with you, I will have nothing to do with him ever again."

"Mr. Dick," said my aunt, "what shall I do with this child?"

Mr. Dick considered, hesitated, then smiled and said, "Have him measured for a suit of clothes."

"Thank you, Mr. Dick," said my aunt. Then turning to her visitors, she said, "Good day, sir. Good day, ma'am. If I ever see you at my door again, I shall knock you down and stamp on you!"

Once they were gone, I ran to Aunt Betsey and threw my arms around her neck and kissed her. Then I shook Mr. Dick's hand and thanked him too.

So I began my new life, with a new name— for my aunt chose to call me Trotwood Copperfield—and with two new guardians with hearts of gold!

"Good Day, Sir. Good Day Ma'am."

"Would You Like To Go to School?"

CHAPTER 6

A New Life

Miss Betsey waited a few weeks until I had recovered from all my suffering. Then one evening while she and Mr. Dick were playing backgammon, she turned to me and said, "Trot," for she had shortened Trotwood to Trot, "we must not forget about your education. Would you like to go to school in Canterbury?"

"I would like that very much," I replied, "for it is so near to here."

The next morning, we got into the cart for the ride to Canterbury. My aunt explained that she was taking me to meet her lawyer,

Mr. Wickfield, for he would be able to advise her as to which school would be best for me.

Miss Betsey stopped the cart before a very old house that seemed to lean into the road. A deathlike face answered our knock. It belonged to a redheaded boy of fifteen who looked years older. His bony skeleton was dressed all in black, and his eyes had no eyebrows and no eyelashes.

"Is Mr. Wickfield at home, Uriah Heep?" my aunt called to the boy.

"Yes, ma'am," he said as he beckoned us inside.

Mr. Wickfield, a handsome old gentleman, met us at his office door. The reddish color of his face and the thickness of his waist reminded me of the men Peggotty used to describe as drinking too much wine. I wondered if this were so with Mr. Wickfield.

"Well, Miss Trotwood, what brings you here?" said Mr. Wickfield pleasantly.

"This is my nephew, David Copperfield,"

Meeting Mr. Wickfield

said Miss Betsey. "I plan to put him into a good school where he will be well taught and well treated. I need your advice on choosing that school."

Mr. Wickfield suggested Dr. Strong's school for boys. Since it was not a boarding school, Mr. Wickfield offered to let me live in his home on weekdays, since I planned to spend my weekends at Aunt Betsey's.

Then I was introduced to Mr. Wickfield's daughter Agnes—a happy, bright-looking girl my age—who loved her father dearly.

Agnes showed me up to the room that was to be mine, and it was as bright and happy as Agnes was. I was eager to unpack and settle myself as soon as my aunt left.

Before I went to bed that night, I met Uriah Heep as he was closing up the office. I offered my hand in friendship. But what a clammy cold hand his was! I rubbed my hand after he had gone, as if trying to warm it and rub his touch away. Something about him

Agnes Shows David up to His Room.

gave me an eerie feeling.

The next morning, I entered on school life again. Mr. Wickfield took me to the school and introduced me to my new master, Doctor Strong, and a pretty young lady the Doctor called Annie. I supposed her to be his daughter and was greatly surprised to hear Mr. Wickfield address her as Mrs. Strong, since the Doctor was a man in his sixties.

In his free time, the Doctor was writing a new Dictionary. One of my classmates, who was bright in mathematics, said he had calculated that at the rate the Doctor was going, he might finish the Dictionary in one thousand six hundred and forty-nine years!

The school was an excellent one, as different from Mr. Creakle's as good is from evil. Dr. Strong was a splendid teacher and was kind to all his boys. They, in turn, loved and respected him and learned their lessons well.

My only discomfort at this time was the constant eerie presence of Uriah Heep!

At Doctor Strong's School

A Serious Talk About David's Career

CHAPTER 7

Visiting Old Friends

How happy I was as my childhood progressed to my youth.

I was seventeen and now the head-boy at school. Doctor Strong referred to me as a "promising young scholar." Agnes Wickfield, a child no more, was now my counselor and my friend. I told her of school, of my dreams, of my loves, of my fights—I told her everything.

As my school days drew to an end, my aunt and I had many serious talks about my career. I had no particular preference for any one career, so my aunt suggested a bit of

DAVID COPPERFIELD

"breathing-time"—a month's change of scene to help me make a clear decision. She suggested that I take a little journey to Yarmouth to see Peggotty, and then go to London for a few days.

I went to Canterbury first to say good-bye to Agnes and Mr. Wickfield. I noticed a change in the old man since I had been there last. His hands trembled, his speech was shaky, and his eyes had a wild look in them. Agnes was worried, almost terrified, about this change in her father as she continued to care for him.

I was heavy at heart when I packed up my books and clothes to be sent to my aunt's house in Dover. Uriah Heep was so anxious to help me with my packing, I thought he was actually glad to see me go.

I boarded the London coach, a well-dressed, well-educated young man with plenty of money in my pockets. How changed I was from the young, weary lad who had traveled

Uriah Heep Is Glad To See David Go.

these same roads years earlier. As we passed Salem House, I had a secret wish to go inside and thrash Mr. Creakle in return for all the thrashings he had given me when I was at his school.

The coach stopped overnight at an inn at Charing Cross. As I sat in the coffee-room after dinner, my eye caught the figure of a handsome, well-dressed young man. I recognized him immediately and called out, "Steerforth! Won't you speak to me?"

"My God!" he exclaimed. "Why it's little Copperfield!"

I was so delighted to see my old school friend, that were I not a young gentleman, I would have hugged him and wept. I brushed away the tears that had managed to creep out, and we sat down together. I told him all that had happened to me over the years since I left Salem House, and he did the same. He had been a student at Oxford University and was now on the way home to

David Recognizes Steerforth.

visit his mother.

"I'm on my way to Yarmouth to visit the Peggottys," I explained, "and then plan to make a decision about my career. It would be great fun if you would join me on my visit."

"Splendid!" said Steerforth. "But if you are in no hurry, why not stop at my home in Highgate for a day or two first?"

"I should like that very much," I replied.

We arrived at Highgate, and I was introduced to an elderly lady with a proud and handsome face. That was Mrs. Steerforth. With her was her companion, Miss Rosa Dartle, a thin, dark-haired young woman with a scar on her lip. Steerforth surprised me when he said *he* was responsible for her scar.

"When I was young, she angered me, and I threw a hammer at her. Some angel I must have been! But she loves me anyway," he said, laughing and raising the glass of wine on the table. "Come, Copperfield, enough of the past. Let us drink to our trip together."

Meeting Mrs. Steerforth and Rosa Dartle

DAVID COPPERFIELD

Steerforth's servant, a respectable-looking man named Littimer, had been working for Steerforth since his university days. During my stay, he waited on both of us. He brought the horses when Steerforth gave me riding lessons; he brought the foils when Steerforth gave me fencing lessons; and he brought gloves when Steerforth taught me to box.

On our arrival in the town of Yarmouth, we checked into a hotel and spent the night. Before I was even up the next morning, Steerforth had already been out strolling the beach, meeting all the boatmen in town.

He came running in excitedly as I was sitting down to breakfast, crying breathlessly, "I'm sure I've seen Mr. Peggotty's boathouse. It's just as you described it. I was almost tempted to walk in and introduce myself as David Copperfield, grown old beyond recognition. But then I decided to let you go to see your old nurse alone first and be cried over for a couple of hours. So go on ahead. I'll join

Steerforth Meets the Boatmen.

you there later, and then we can go up to the boathouse together."

It had been seven years since Peggotty had seen me, even though I had written to her constantly all that time. So when she came to answer my knock at her cottage door, she asked politely, "What are you wanting, sir?"

In my best rough voice, I answered, "I'd like some information about a house in Blunderstone—the Copperfield house."

Peggotty took a step back and her hands flew to her face. "My darling boy!" she cried.

"My Peggotty!" I cried to her. And we both burst into tears, locked in each other's arms.

Barkis was ill in bed with rheumatism, but he greeted me almost as enthusiastically as Peggotty did. We spent several hours talking about the old times when I carried his "Barkis is willin'" messages.

Steerforth joined us a while later, and his easy, spirited good humor, fine manners, and handsome looks won Peggotty's heart in

"My Darling Boy!"

minutes.

At eight o'clock, we started for the boat-house to see Mr. Peggotty, Emily, and Ham.

The door was unlatched, so we quietly entered. Mr. Peggotty was sitting by the fire. Emily and Ham were opposite him, their hands locked in each others, talking excitedly about something that brought joy to the old man's face and had Mrs. Gummidge clapping her hands wildly.

The next instant, Ham was on his feet, crying, "It's Mas'r Davy!"

Everyone jumped up, and we were all shaking hands and talking at once and laughing. We soon joined them at the fire, and Ham told us with a blush that he and Emily were to be married. We congratulated them and then talked and laughed over Steerforth's stories for hours. Emily's eyes were fastened on Steerforth all the while he was talking, and soon she mustered up enough courage to

Laughing over Steerforth's Stories

join in our conversation.

Steerforth was quite taken with the family and especially with Emily, but he did remark later when we were alone that Ham seemed to be too much of a blockhead for her.

I was shocked at this cold remark, but seeing a laughing twinkle in his eye, I decided he was just joking.

We stayed in Yarmouth for more than a fortnight. Steerforth went boating often with Mr. Peggotty while I went back several times to visit my childhood home at Blunderstone. There were great changes there. The Murdstones no longer lived in the house. The garden had run wild, and half the windows of the house were shut up. The graves beneath the tree where both my parents and my tiny half-brother lay brought feelings of sadness to me.

One evening when I returned from one of my trips to Blunderstone, I found Steerforth alone in Mr. Peggotty's house. His face was

David Visits His Childhood Home.

dark as he sat staring at the fire. When he saw me, he raised his head.

"I've bought a boat," he said, with his usual good-natured smile returning to his face. "Mr. Peggotty will master it for me while I'm away. Littimer will come down to see to new sails and to have the boat renamed. I'm calling her the *Little Emily.*"

With Steerforth having such good news, I couldn't understand why he had been sitting at the fire with such a scowl on his face.... And why did he name the boat the *Little Emily*?

At Peggotty's house later that night, I met a friend of Emily's. Her name was Martha, and she and Emily had known each other since they were children. Martha was in some kind of trouble and had come to Emily for help. Emily wept as she heard Martha's story. Then she gave the poor girl what money she could so that Martha could go to London and begin her life again.

Martha Comes to Emily for Help.

Steerforth and David Leave Yarmouth.

CHAPTER 8

I Choose a Career

Steerforth and I left Yarmouth the next day. Peggotty and her family saw us off, and many seafaring men who had become Steerforth's friends came to bid him good-bye.

For a time, Steerforth and I held no conversation in the coach. After a while, Steerforth said, "Now that you've had breathing time, have you decided on a career?"

"Not exactly," I replied. "I had thought about becoming a proctor—a business agent."

Steerforth then told me all he knew about proctors and that occupation.

We parted that day, Steerforth to go to

Highgate and I to meet Aunt Betsey in London at the hotel where she was staying.

Once there, I told my aunt about my plans. "But," I added, "I am worried that the proctor training might cost too much."

She took my hands in hers and said gently, "Trot, perhaps I might have been better friends with your poor father when he was alive and with your poor mother when you were only a small child. But it is too late to regret that. And I am long over the disappointment of your being born David, rather than the Betsey I had hoped for. Then, Trot, you came to me. Your love and your caring have done more for me than this old woman could ever do for you."

I thanked Aunt Betsey with my eyes wet with tears. And even though I was a man of seventeen, I did not mind her warm hug.

The next day, we set out for the office of Spenlow and Jorkins, my aunt's proctors. They had an opening for a proctor-in-training,

David Thanks Aunt Betsey.

DAVID COPPERFIELD

and they had agreed to take me on for a month's trial. Then my aunt and I left to look for furnished rooms for me. We found rooms at the top floor of a house overlooking the river.

It was a wonderfully fine thing to have that lofty castle to myself, to walk about town with a key to my house in my pocket. Only at night did I become lonely. I wanted somebody to talk to then, and I thought of Agnes and the days I lived at the Wickfields'. How I missed her!

Next day, a note came from Agnes. She was visiting friends in London with her father and Uriah Heep, and she wanted to see me. I hurried to her hotel that very afternoon.

Agnes greeted me warmly, but I could see that something was troubling her. Then she explained that Uriah Heep had persuaded her father to take him in as a partner in his business. At first, Agnes had thought that

106

Furnished Rooms for David

her father would have less to worry about
with Heep helping him, but now she feared
that Heep was taking advantage of the old
man. For Mr. Wickfield seemed to be com-
pletely in Heep's power.

Agnes began to weep, and I comforted her
as best I could. By the time Mr. Wickfield and
Heep joined us for dinner, she was more com-
posed. Later in the evening, when Agnes left
to take her father to bed, Heep took me aside
and told me some startling news—he was in
love with Agnes and wanted to marry her! I
had the wild idea of seizing the red-hot poker
from the fireplace and running it through
him. I could never let this wretch marry my
dear Agnes. Never! Besides, I suspected that
his reasons were more than love—if it were
possible for such a wretched creature to love.
No, I told myself, he's interested in the Wickfield business as well. I couldn't wait to get
away from him that evening, and I left after
Agnes rejoined us.

Heep Marry Agnes? Never!

Mr. Spenlow, my new employer, invited me to his country home for a weekend to celebrate my employment with his firm. There, I met Dora, his daughter. She was the loveliest creature on earth, and I fell in love immediately. The weekend proved to be one of the most beautiful of my life, and I left there more in love with Dora than when I had first set eyes on her.

Back in London I was invited to dinner at the home of some business friends. Other guests were there too, but one attracted my attention when I heard his name, even before he came in. The name was Mr. Traddles.

My mind flew back to my school days at Salem House. Could it be the same Tommy Traddles who had introduced me to the other boys when I had to wear my sign? The same Tommy Traddles who used to make the sound effects when I was telling Steerforth all my stories? . . . I looked among the guests for Mr. Traddles. He was pointed out to me as the

David Falls in Love.

sober young man standing off in a corner. The comic head of hair and wide-open eyes convinced me. It *was* Tommy!

I hurried over to him and introduced myself. How joyfully he greeted me! We made plans to get together for a visit at his home the very next day.

I found the street he had written down for me. It was a sloppy, untidy street with garbage piled in the gutter. The place reminded me of the days when I lived in such a place with Mr. and Mrs. Micawber.

Traddles was on the landing and welcomed me into his neat little room heartily. We talked of old times at Mr. Creakle's and what we had been doing since then. Tommy's parents were dead, and the uncle with whom he had lived had died, leaving him nothing. He now struggled as a law student and took odd jobs to support himself. And he was engaged to Sophy, his "dearest girl in the world," but he feared it would be a long engagement

Finding Traddles' Address

because of his financial circumstances.

Engagement! Oh, how I thought of Dora and envied Tommy!

Tommy went on, "I don't make much, but I don't spend much. I board with the people downstairs, and they are very kind indeed. Yes, both Mr. and Mrs. Micawber have had hard times in life."

"Micawber!" I exclaimed. "I know them well. I must go down and see them."

I ran down the stairs and was soon greeting Mr. and Mrs. Micawber. At first they didn't recognize me, but after I introduced myself, we talked of old times. They invited me to dinner, but I saw that they could hardly afford to feed another mouth, so I quickly set a date for Tommy and the Micawbers to come and dine with me.

My dinner party went well, and after my guests had gone, I sat down by the fire recalling the pleasant hours spent with my newfound old friends. Suddenly, I heard a quick

Greeting Mr. and Mrs. Micawber

step on the stairs. My door was flung open and there stood James Steerforth!

Steerforth had just come from Yarmouth, where he had been sailing in his new boat. In answer to all my questions, Steerforth filled me in on the news of my friends there.

"No, Emily and Ham are not married yet," he said, "and Barkis, the carriage driver, is quite ill and seems about to take his last journey."

"Then I must go to Peggotty immediately," I said. "She might need me to comfort her during her husband's last days."

"Why not come to Highgate first?" suggested Steerforth. "I'm on the way there. I haven't seen my mother in a long while. Besides, who knows when we may meet again otherwise?"

That was a strange way to offer me an invitation, I thought, but I agreed to go.

So, on my way to Yarmouth, I stopped at Highgate. Miss Dartle, Mrs. Steerforth's

An Unexpected Visitor

companion, greeted me with an even stranger question. "Are you the one who has been keeping James away from home for such long periods of time?" she asked.

I was honestly confused. "I know nothing of Steerforth's affairs," I replied, "or where he spends his time. Last night was the first time I have seen him in a long while."

All this time, Steerforth was watching me closely, as if he had something on his mind. But he said nothing of it.

Before going to bed that night, I told him I would be leaving the next morning before he awoke. He held my shoulders and seemed unwilling to let me go. "David," he said, "if anything should ever part us, you must think of me at my best."

"You have no best and no worst," I replied. "You will always be loved as my dear friend." But I did think that his words were strange. Still, I quickly put them out of my mind in my concern for Peggotty.

"You Must Think of Me at My Best."

Sad About Barkis' Illness

CHAPTER 9

A Great Loss

I reached Peggotty's house in Yarmouth in the evening. My low tap at the door was answered by Mr. Peggotty. He led me into the kitchen where Emily was sitting by the fire, sad and quiet. Ham was standing near her, but she seemed to be trying to avoid his arm on her shoulder. Ham told me that they were to be quietly married in a fortnight.

I sat counting the ticking of the clock. Soon Peggotty came down, looking tired and worn. She took me in her arms and asked me to come upstairs. There, in the bedroom, lay Barkis, mute and senseless.

"He's going out with the tide," whispered Mr. Peggotty. "People along the coast only die when the tide's almost out."

We remained there with Barkis for several hours. He opened his eyes once and tried to stretch out his arm to me.

"Barkis is willin'!" he gasped with a slight smile. Then he went out with the tide.

After the funeral, we went our ways, planning to meet in Mr. Peggotty's old boathouse that evening. The day passed slowly.

Rain was falling heavily, but there was a moon behind the clouds, so it was not dark as I made my way to the barge. Peggotty, Mrs. Gummidge, and Mr. Peggotty were there when I arrived.

Ham entered a while later, alone.

"Where's Emily?" asked Mr. Peggotty.

Ham made a motion with his hand, as if she were outside. Then he turned to me, deadly pale, and said, "Mas'r Davy, will you come out a minute and see what Emily and

"Barkis Is Willin'!"

me has got to show you?"

We went out. Ham shut the door, and we were alone.

"Emily's run away," he said grimly, and he began to weep. "How can I tell Mr. Peggotty?"

It was too late to wonder, for the door opened and Mr. Peggotty stepped out. One look at Ham's pale face, and he knew.

As we went back inside, Ham explained that Emily had left a note. She had left to become a lady, and if the man she had run away with didn't make her one, she could never return home.

"Who's the man?" asked Mr. Peggotty, his face white and trembling.

Ham glanced at me, silent for a moment. I felt a shock—I had guessed—and I sank down in a chair.

"There's been a servant about here," Ham said, faltering, "and his gen'lm'an too."

I felt Peggotty's arm round my neck as

"Emily's Run Away."

Ham went on to describe Littimer and Steerforth. I could not have uttered a sound or moved if the house had been about to fall in.

"Don't tell me his name's Steerforth!" boomed Mr. Peggotty.

But Ham turned to me and, in a broken voice, said, "It ain't no fault of yourn, Mas'r Davy. But his name *is* Steerforth, and he's a damned villain!"

I did not ask their pardon; I did not curse Steerforth; I only cried. I held my friend's memory dear, but I felt as he had felt the last night I saw him—that all was ended between us. That was probably what Steerforth had meant the day before at Highgate when he said, "If anything should ever part us, you must think of me at my best."

There was no comforting Mr. Peggoty.

"I'm leaving now to find my niece. If I have to search the whole world," he cried wildly, "I will. As for *him,* I should have drowned him when he was out on my boat!"

There Was No Comforting Mr. Peggotty.

At Dora's Birthday Party

CHAPTER 10

Ruined!

Taking the management of Peggotty's affairs into my own hands, I settled Barkis' will and soon got everything in order for her.

Mr. Spenlow invited me to a picnic in honor of Dora's birthday. I brought Dora flowers, which she kept with her all during the picnic. She gaily tried to get her little dog Jip to smell them, but he growled and refused to. With Dora, I felt totally happy.

Four days later, Dora and I were engaged, but we decided to keep it a secret from her father for a while. However, I told Peggotty, who was still in London on the will business, and I wrote to Agnes about it.

Returning to my rooms with Peggotty one day, we were surprised to find my door open and to hear voices inside. We looked at one another and went into the sitting-room. To my amazement, I found, of all people upon earth, my aunt and Mr. Dick! My aunt was sitting on her luggage drinking tea, with her two birds by her and her cat on her knee. Mr. Dick was leaning thoughtfully on a great kite with more luggage about him.

"My dear Aunt!" I cried, embracing her. "What an unexpected pleasure!"

I knew my aunt well enough to know that she had something important on her mind for her to come to London. Had she learned of my engagement to Dora before I told her? Had I offended her in some way? I had no way of knowing. But I knew she would speak only in her own good time.

Finally, when my aunt had finished her tea, she spoke. "Trot," she said, "why do you

An Unexpected Pleasure

think I'm sitting here on my luggage?"

I shook my head, unable to guess.

"Because," said my aunt, "it's all I have. Because I'm ruined, my dear! All I have in the world is in this room except the cottage in Dover which is being rented. We must not let this frighten us, my dear. We must live down misfortune, Trot! And you must be strong and self-reliant."

I could hardly have received a greater shock.

"Dick knows it," continued my aunt, laying her hand calmly on my shoulder. "We will need a bed for Dick tonight. Perhaps, to save expenses, you can make up a bed here for me. Anything will do. It's just for tonight."

As soon as I recovered from my amazement at my aunt's words, I suggested a place I knew of where Mr. Dick could rent a room.

As it was growing late, I led Mr. Dick to the rooming house. He was carrying his great kite at his back.

David Leads Mr. Dick to a Rooming House.

When I had him settled, I returned to my rooms to find my aunt pacing up and down. She told me that she and Peggotty had been talking about my engagement to Dora.

"So you fancy yourself in love?" she said.

"Fancy, Aunt!" I exclaimed, as red as I could be. "I adore Dora with my whole soul! We are young, I know. And perhaps we might appear foolish to others. But we love each other truly."

Aunt Betsey smiled sadly and muttered, "Well, it may come to nothing. But then there's time one of these days for it to come to something."

I was pleased, at least, that there was a small bit of affection in her words. So I thanked her for all her kindnesses to me and went to bed.

But I could not sleep, wondering miserably if my poor circumstances would change Mr. Spenlow's mind about permitting Dora to marry me . . . when we told him, that is.

"I Adore Dora with My Whole Soul."

Since I was earning nothing while I was getting my proctor training, how would I court Dora and still help my aunt too?

The next day was no better. I faced Mr. Spenlow and his partner, Mr. Jorkins, and explained my financial problem—that I would have to cancel my training, which my aunt had been paying for. Neither man offered to let me stay on or even to return the thousand pounds my aunt had advanced to them for my training.

As I walked home from the office, trying to plan for the worst money shortages, a hackney cab stopped at my feet. I looked up and saw the one face that always brought a happy smile to my face—Agnes!

"Oh, Agnes!" I cried. "What a pleasure to see you! If I could have had one wish, it would have been to talk to you."

She got out of the cab and as we walked, she explained that she had come to London to see my aunt after learning of her financial

A Cab Stops near David.

problems, for Agnes and Aunt Betsey had been very fond of each other these many years. She was with her father and Uriah Heep. Agnes sadly told me how she had little chance to be alone with her father now, or even alone herself, for Uriah Heep had not only become Mr. Wickfield's business partner, but had moved into their house as well.

"Trot, I fear that Heep is planning some fraud or treachery against my father," she added, trembling. "Yet I pray that I am mistaken."

When we arrived at my rooms, Miss Betsey welcomed Agnes lovingly and began confiding our misfortunes to her. And for the first time I learned exactly what had happened to my aunt's money. It seems she had invested in some bank stock upon the advice of the firm of Wickfield and Heep. But the bank failed, and all the investors lost everything.

"I must do something'" I cried.

"What?" Aunt Betsey said with alarm. "Go

Agnes Confides Her Fears to Aunt Betsey.

to sea or join the army? I won't hear of it. You are going to finish your studies and become a proctor and then perhaps a lawyer."

All this time Agnes had been listening, pale and breathless. Finally she spoke. "Perhaps, David, you could continue your training and work in your free time. I know that your old favorite teacher, Dr. Strong, is in London now and is looking for a secretary to help him on the Dictionary he is still writing. Would you mind that work?"

"Dear Agnes!" I cried. "Mind? What would I do without you? You were always my good angel."

"Dora is your good angel now," she reminded me with a laugh.

How delighted I was with the idea of earning my own money! And I immediately wrote to Doctor Strong, asking for an appointment.

The next day I went to call upon Doctor Strong. I found him walking in his garden.

"Why, Copperfield," he said, "you are a

"Why, Copperfield, You Are a Man!"

man!"

After we chatted for a while about family and old friends, he became serious. "You were a fine student, Copperfield," he began. "You are qualified for many things. Why would you want to take such an unimportant job as my secretary? It only pays seventy pounds a year."

"It would double our income," I replied. "And I could go on with my studies while working for you in my free time."

"All right," said Doctor Strong. "But you must promise that if you find a better job, you will take it."

"On my word, sir."

"Fine, fine," said the Doctor.

We arranged that I would work two hours every morning and three hours every night, except on Saturdays and Sundays when I was to rest.

So I began my busy schedule, up at five in the morning and home at nine or ten at

A Busy Work Schedule

night.

Mr. Dick had begun to fret because he felt useless and couldn't help Aunt Betsey. I then recalled my old friend Tommy Traddles and thought perhaps he might have some ideas or business connections to help Mr. Dick. And Traddles did.

He, himself, would be able to use Mr. Dick, who wrote with extraordinary neatness, to copy legal documents. And he even had a suggestion for me. He said that if I could learn shorthand, I would be able to get a job reporting the debates in Parliament for the newspapers.

During our visit, Traddles had other news for me. It was a letter from our old friend, Mr. Micawber, whom Traddles had been helping with several loans of money. Mr. Micawber wrote that he now had a job in Canterbury, working as a confidential law clerk ... to Uriah Heep! I sat amazed and a bit worried, for I did not trust Uriah Heep.

Mr. Dick Copies Legal Papers for Traddles.

Peggotty Leaves for Yarmouth.

CHAPTER 11

My Dear Dora

The time had now come for Peggotty to return to Yarmouth. She had heard nothing from her brother since he had gone off in search of Emily, and she now wanted to return home to care for Ham. Before she boarded her coach, she made me promise that if ever I needed money, I was to come to her. I assured her that I would.

I then went to Dora's house and asked her if she could love a beggar, because I now was one. She shook her curls and laughed.

Dora's childish ways were delicious to me, yet I had to make her understand. "But Dora, my dear," I cried, "I am your ruined David. Is your heart still mine?"

"Oh, yes!" cried Dora. "But don't go on with your dreadful talk about being poor."

"Indeed I will not, my darling," I assured her. "But it would be useful to us afterwards if you could read a cook book and learn to keep household accounts."

Dora half-cried, half-screamed at my words, and I thought I had killed her. But I calmed her after a while. My dear Dora was a lovely child, frightened of facing the real world and its problems.

As I left, Dora said, "Now don't get up at five o'clock, you naughty boy. It's so silly."

"I have work to do, my love."

"Then don't do it!" she said.

It was impossible to tell that sweet little face that we must work to live. She laughed, and I loved her.

I worked at my shorthand for the Parliamentary debates and had dreams of curves

"I Have Work To Do."

and marks like flies' legs. It was like learning a new alphabet.

The harmony of these days was shattered by an accident. Mr. Spenlow was thrown from his horse and killed. Dora went to live with her aunts in Putney, and I didn't see her.

I was in a terrible state of depression when Aunt Betsey sent me to Dover to check on the tenants renting her cottage.

Everything was in order at the cottage, and on the way back to London, I stopped at Canterbury to visit Agnes and Mr. Wickfield. Uriah Heep's presence in the house made me most uncomfortable, and I had no time alone with Agnes my first afternoon.

After dinner I sat with the men. Heep encouraged Mr. Wickfield to drink more than he should. I kept silent.

Suddenly Uriah Heep blurted out, "Mr. Wickfield, I've an ambition to make your Agnes my Agnes. I want to be her husband."

Mr. Wickfield rose from the table with a

The Men Sat After Dinner.

cry. He seemed to go mad for the moment, tearing at his hair, beating his head, and staring wildly, speechless. I put my arms around him to steady him.

"Look at him," Mr. Wickfield finally said, pointing to Heep. "My torturer! He has taken my good reputation and smeared it. He has taken my peace and quiet, and even my house and home. Marry Agnes? Never!"

"That is the wine talking," cried Heep. "You'll change your mind tomorrow."

Just then Agnes came into the room and led her father up to bed. Later, she joined me as I sat alone. She had been weeping, but her face was still very beautiful.

"Dearest Agnes," I said gently, "you are my dearest friend, and I love you. You must not marry Uriah Heep, not for the sake of your father's business nor for any other reason. You are too good for a man like him!"

She smiled and said only, "I must trust in God." And then she was gone.

Mr. Wickfield Seems To Go Mad.

After I returned home, I wrote to Dora's aunts, asking if I might visit. The reply was "yes," on Saturdays and Sundays.

And so began glorious days for me. I threw myself into my work and my studies, looking forward to my weekend visits with Dora.

But I was distressed to see Dora's aunts treat her like a plaything. They waited on her, curled her hair, and made ornaments for her. This made Dora happy, but I didn't feel that treating her like a child would help prepare her for our life together.

I was delighted one day when Dora asked me to give her a cook book and show her how to keep household accounts. But the cook book made Dora's head ache, and the numbers made her cry because they wouldn't add up.

Therefore, both books were put in the corner of the room for Jip to stand on, which Dora trained him to do. She was so delighted at this that I was glad I had bought them.

Dora Uses the Books for Jip's Tricks.

David Sees a Man on the Church Steps.

CHAPTER 12

Mr. Peggotty, the Wanderer

I left work at Doctor Strong's one snowy night to walk home. The noise of wheels and the steps of people were as hushed as if the streets had been covered with feathers. I took the shortest way home—through St. Martin's Lane. At the corner I saw a woman's face. It looked at me, then disappeared. But I recognized that face. It was Martha, Martha Endell, Emily's friend—the woman Emily had once given money to.

Then on the steps of St. Martin's Church I saw a man stooped over to adjust a bundle he was carrying. As he straightened up, I saw his face and he saw mine. It was ... Mr. Peggotty! We shook hands heartily, both of us speechless for a moment.

"Mas'r Davy!" he finally cried, gripping my arm. "It does my heart good to see you, sir."

"My dear old friend!" I cried. "Let us get out of the snow and get something hot to drink." I put my arm through his and we went to an inn.

In the light I saw he was grayer. The lines in his face and forehead were deeper. He told me he had been following Emily on foot to France, then to Italy, then over the mountains in Switzerland. As he talked, I saw the door open and a drift of snow blow in. Then I spied Martha at the door. I saw her tired face, listening carefully. I hoped Mr. Peggotty hadn't seen her, for he had never approved of Martha's friendship with Emily. And seeing her might upset the old man! Besides, Martha was motioning to me with her hands not to betray her.

Martha Listens To a Conversation.

"The dear child sends money to Mrs. Gummidge for me, but she gives no address," Mr. Peggotty sobbed. He hadn't touched any of the money, and he showed me the letters and the money to prove it. And now he was on his way again, this time to Germany—where Emily's last letter was postmarked.

"And Ham?" I asked. "How is he?"

Mr. Peggotty shook his head. "He works hard and doesn't complain, but this has hurt him deeply." Mr. Peggotty gathered up his letters and placed them tenderly in his breast pocket. Then he rose to go.

I looked toward the door, but Martha was gone. As I left the inn, I saw that the snow had covered all footprints. My new tracks were the only ones to be seen. And even they began to die away in the falling snow as I walked toward home.

The Snow Covered All Footprints.

A Light in Doctor Strong's Study

CHAPTER 13

The Evil Uriah Heep

Agnes and her father came to visit Doctor Strong for several days, the two men being old friends. Naturally, Heep came along. One night when I was finishing work, I saw a light in the Doctor's study. I went in to say goodnight and to scold him for working so late on the Dictionary without me. I found Uriah Heep there with the Doctor and Mr. Wickfield. The Doctor had his face covered with his hands, and Mr. Wickfield looked drawn and pained. I wondered what could have happened.

"I have told the Doctor of the goings-on of

Mrs. Strong," said Heep, "of his dear Annie's interest in another man."

I could not believe Heep's cruelty. His story was not true, of course, but the old Doctor believed it because his lovely wife was so much younger than he. He thought she might have married him because he was a wealthy man. I couldn't bear it. Heep was a liar and a cheat and seemed to be trying to bring sadness to everyone.

Then to Mr. Wickfield, Heep added, "And to think that your dear Agnes has been such a close friend to Mrs. Strong! Surely Copperfield here, who has been working so closely with the Doctor, must have noticed all these goings-on."

"You villain!" I cried in a rage. "How dare you trap me in your evil scheme!" I couldn't bear it any longer, and I struck Heep's cheek so hard, my fingers burned. "You may go to the devil!" I cried and ran from the house.

Over the next few weeks, I noticed a

The Doctor and Mr. Wickfield Were Sad.

change in the once-happy Strongs. The Doctor looked older, and Annie seemed always to have hurt and confused tears in her eyes. The house grew quiet.

The only relief came in the visits by Mr. Dick. He walked up and down the garden with the Doctor and talked to Mrs. Strong. He became what no one else could be—a link between them.

During the Wickfields' visit, Uriah Heep received many business letters from Mr. Micawber, his clerk. I was somewhat surprised to receive a letter from Mrs. Micawber at this time. She was distressed that her husband had become secretive and distant from her and from their children. He, who had once been a loving husband and devoted father, was now cold and severe. She appealed to me for advice, but I could suggest only kindness and patience to win her husband back.

But her letter set me to thinking.

A Distressing Letter from Mrs. Micawber

David and Dora Are Married.

CHAPTER 14

My Child-Wife

Weeks, months, and seasons pass along. I reached the legal age of twenty-one and Dora and I were married.

I doubt whether two young birds could have known less about housekeeping than Dora and I. We had a servant to keep house for us, but we had an awful time with her. Dinner was late or never served at all. Our meat was always red raw or burnt to ashes. Pieces of our silver disappeared. And Dora could not bring herself to scold the woman.

So, rather than have any more arguments with my dear Dora, I took care of all these tasks in our scrambled household myself, and Dora lived her cheerful life.

My aunt and Dora had become close friends. Miss Betsey urged me to have patience in these household matters, but when I asked her to advise Dora how to run a house, she refused.

"These are early days, Trot," she told me. "You have married a very pretty and affectionate girl. It is your duty to judge her by the qualities she has, and not by the qualities she may not have. Try, instead, to develop these qualities in her. And if you cannot, then simply do without them. Your future is between you two—you must work your problems out yourselves in a marriage."

I kissed my aunt and thanked her for her good advice.

I worked hard at my studies and my work and began to do some writing in my spare time in the evenings. My stories sold well, and I gladly gave up my work with Doctor

Dora's Cheerful Life

Strong. Although I loved my "child-wife" (as Dora wished to be called), I did sometimes yearn for a wife with more character, who could share my work and my interests more. But this was never meant to be. I was happy, but it was not the happiness I had hoped for. Something was missing. But Dora was bright and cheerful and happy with our life.

As the year wore on, Dora seemed to be losing what little strength she had. My child-wife was not becoming a woman. She looked very pretty and was very merry. But the little feet that used to be so nimble when they danced around Jip were now dull and motionless.

I began to carry her downstairs every morning and upstairs every night. Jip would bark and caper round us. My aunt, the best of nurses, followed us with a mass of shawls and pillows. Sometimes, when I picked Dora up and felt that she was lighter in my arms, a frightening, blank feeling came upon me.

Dora Grows Weak.

"Could You Speak to Me, Trotwood?"

CHAPTER 15

Mr. Dick Saves a Marriage

It had been a long time since I had worked for Doctor Strong. But living in his neighborhood, I saw him often. Uriah Heep's cruel words had taken hold of his heart and tortured him continually. He had grown more and more dismal and quiet.

One night, Mr. Dick put his head into the parlor and asked, "Could you speak to me, Trotwood?"

"Certainly, Mr. Dick," I said. "Come in."

"Now, boy," he began, "I am going to ask you a question. What do you think of me in this respect?" And he touched his forehead.

DAVID COPPERFIELD

I was puzzled how to answer, but he helped me. "I am simple and weak-minded," he said. "I know I am, though your aunt pretends I am not. If she hadn't been my friend and taken care of me all these years, I would have been locked up because I *am* so simple. But, sir, even a simple man can see clouds."

"What clouds?" I asked.

"The clouds between Annie and Doctor Strong," he replied. "Why are they there?"

I explained as simply as I could what Uriah Heep had done.

"But why can't Miss Betsey, the most wonderful woman in the world, or a scholar like yourself help?"

"It is too delicate a subject," I said. "We cannot interfere."

"Well, sir," said Mr. Dick, "a poor, simple fellow who appears crazy like me may do what wonderful or scholarly people dare not. *I'll* bring them together. They wouldn't blame *me* for interfering. I'm only Mr. Dick. And

Mr. Dick Wants To Help the Strongs.

who pays any attention to Mr. Dick? I have been thinking about it for some time, and I now have an idea."

I heard no more about it for two weeks, and I was convinced that in his unsettled state of mind, Mr. Dick had forgotten the whole matter. Then one evening, Mr. Dick led Annie, pale and trembling, into the Doctor's study while we were there on a visit.

Annie knelt at the Doctor's feet and sobbed. "Oh, my husband, I beg you to break this long silence. Tell me what trouble has come between us."

"Annie, my dear," said the Doctor, tenderly taking her hand, "the change in our lives is my fault. But there is no change in the love and respect I have for you."

"But something is wrong. I know it in my heart. If you will not speak, then let one of my friends here do so." And she looked around at Mr. Dick, my aunt, and me.

After a long silence, I began, painfully,

Annie Sobs at the Doctor's Feet.

hesitatingly, telling her of Uriah Heep's cruel story. When I had finished, Annie kissed the Doctor's hand and spoke softly to him.

"When I was a young girl, I was deeply, fondly attached to you as a father. Then, although your wish to marry me came as a surprise, I was proud that you thought me worthy of you. Then as a husband, you were so good and kind that I grew to love you in a far different way. There has never been another man. I have never wronged you."

"Annie, my dear!" cried the Doctor, taking her in his arms.

In the silence that followed, my aunt leaned over and kissed Mr. Dick. "You are a very remarkable man, Dick," she said, "and never pretend to be anything else, for I know better."

When Mr. Dick, my aunt, and I left the Strongs' house, Annie had her arms around the Doctor's neck, and her dark brown curls were mixed with his gray hair.

"You Are a Very Remarkable Man."

Mrs. Steerforth Questions David.

CHAPTER 16

I Am Involved in Two Mysteries

One evening as I was returning from a walk, I passed Mrs. Steerforth's house. A maid called to me, asking me to come in.

"Has Emily been found?" asked Mrs. Steerforth angrily when I entered.

"No," I replied in amazement. "Isn't she with James?"

"She has run away from my son," she said with a laugh. "Perhaps she'll never be found. Perhaps she's dead!"

"What do you know of Emily?" I asked. "Her family and friends are very worried."

"She was in Europe with James and his

DAVID COPPERFIELD

servant, Littimer," Mrs. Steerforth explained. "For a while, James was quite taken with her. She spoke the languages of all the countries they visited and was much admired wherever they went. Then she became depressed, and James grew tired of her. He left her in Italy, with the suggestion that she marry Littimer, a man of her own station."

"Oh, Emily! Unhappy child!" I thought.

"Well, after James left, Emily became violent and had to be locked in her room. But she climbed out a window and was gone. She may have drowned herself, for she had threatened to. At any rate, she's gone and has not been seen or heard of since. James is sailing Spain's coast at the moment."

"Then what do you want of me?" I asked.

"I called you in to see if you knew where that wretched girl is. I do not want my son falling into her hands again!"

"Madam," I said respectfully, "I assure you, having known Emily's family since childhood,

Emily Climbed Out a Window.

that she would never take anything from your son." With that, I turned and left.

The following evening, I went to London to look for Mr. Peggotty. He was always wandering, but I had seen him in London, searching the streets and doorways for Emily.

When I reached his room and told him the news, he turned pale.

"Do you think she's alive?" he asked me in a frightened voice.

"Yes," I said, "and if she has made her way back to London, I believe there is one person she might contact—her friend Martha. And I know that Martha is in London, for I saw her outside the tavern the last time I met you."

"I've seen her in the streets too," said Mr. Peggotty. "But why would Emily go to her? I always thought Emily was too good for that girl."

"Because Emily once helped Martha before she left home," I explained.

"I might know where to look for Martha,"

David Tells Mr. Peggotty the News.

said Mr. Peggotty. "Let's go."

We were not far from Blackfriars Bridge when he turned and pointed to a figure walking alone. We followed her to a desolate area near the river. Coarse grass and weeds straggled over the marshy land. Frames of houses, begun and never finished, stood rotting away. The ground was covered with parts of steam boilers, discarded pipes, wheels, furnaces, boats sunk into the ground, and other strange objects. My body shook; the place had an eerie air about it.

The girl we were following stopped and stood, lonely and still, amid this decaying refuse, looking at the water. I was sure she meant to drown herself. I started toward her and grabbed her arm. "Martha!" I cried.

She uttered a scream and struggled with me. Mr. Peggotty grasped her other arm. When she finally recognized us, she slumped between us, and we carried her away from the water.

Finding Martha near the River

She cried hysterically for a long while, but when she was calm, I told her of Emily.

"She was always good to me!" cried Martha. "When she ran away, I feared that people would think she had gone bad because of her association with me. Oh, how I would gladly die to bring back Emily's good name!"

Mr. Peggotty looked at the pleading woman on the ground. He put her shawl around her shoulders and helped her to her feet. "Martha," he said, "I have gone almost to the world's farthest end to find my dear niece. I love her, but she's filled with shame. Mas'r Davy and I believe she'll come to London one day. Help us find her, please."

Martha lifted her eyes and swore, "I'll devote myself faithfully to this task. If I find her, I'll care for her and let you know immediately."

About this time, Traddles and I began receiving alarming letters from the Micawbers. Then Mr. Micawber himself appeared, his

David Tells Martha About Emily.

face clouded and his eyes weary.

"Gentlemen," he said to Traddles and me, "you are friends in need. You are looking at a wreck of a man. My mind is troubled, and I have lost my self respect. And it is all because of the villainy, deception, fraud, and conspiracy of . . . HEEP!"

Micawber was raving. "I will lead this life no longer! I have been under an evil spell in that infernal scoundrel's service. I will blow to fragments that detestable serpent—Heep! I will cause Mount Vesuvius to erupt on that rascal—Heep! I will choke the eyes out of the head of that cheat and liar—Heep! I must expose that doomed traitor—Heep!"

I feared Mr. Micawber would die on the spot, he was so angry and flustered. Finally, he fell into a chair to catch his breath. He asked Traddles, Aunt Betsey, Mr. Dick, and me to meet him at a Canterbury hotel in a week. He would bring the proof that would expose Heep! Then he rushed out of the house.

"I Must Expose That Doomed Traitor!"

Martha Appears at David's Garden Gate.

CHAPTER 17

Mr. Peggotty's Dream Comes True

It had been months since Mr. Peggotty and I had found Martha on the bank of the river. I began to give up hope of ever finding Emily alive. But Mr. Peggotty's hope and patience never faltered.

One evening I was in the garden when Martha appeared at the gate.

"Can you come with me?" she whispered. "I have been to Mr. Peggotty's, but he is not at home. I wrote down where he was to come and left it on his table. Can you come now?"

I went out the garden gate immediately, and we turned towards London. I hired a passing coach, and once she gave the driver the address, she sat back silently. We reached Golden Square—an area where once-costly homes had become poor lodgings with rooms rented out. Stopping at one of these lodgings, Martha beckoned me to follow her up the staircase. We climbed to the top story of the house.

There was a dead silence for some minutes as we waited. Then I heard a distant footstep on the stairs. Mr. Peggotty passed by me and rushed into the room.

"Uncle!" cried Emily's soft voice.

A fearful cry followed the word, and as I looked into the room, I saw Mr. Peggotty holding the unconscious Emily in his arms.

"Mas'r Davy," he said in a low, hoarse voice, "I thank the Heavenly Father for making my dream come true!" Then he picked up the motionless girl and carried her down the stairs.

The next morning, Mr. Peggotty called on

Mr. Peggotty Holds Emily in His Arms.

me as my aunt and I were in the garden. He told us how Emily had run away from Steerforth's servant and had been hidden and cared for by a kind woman who lived near them on the beach. "Emily became ill with fever," Mr. Peggotty explained, "but the woman nursed her back to health. When she was strong again, she left for London. What little money she had she gave to the kind woman." Mr. Peggotty's eyes filled with tears, but he went on. "She worked at inns in Italy and France to earn her passage to England, but all the while fearing to see me. It was in London that Martha found her and told her how I still loved her."

I was silent, but Aunt Betsey was sobbing. Then I asked Mr. Peggotty, "And what are you planning for your future, good friend?"

"I'm taking Emily to Australia. We can build a new life there."

"And when do you plan to leave?" I asked.

"As soon as I can take my farewell leave of

"I'm Taking Emily to Australia."

Yarmouth and settle the boathouse. Mas'r Davy, could you do me the kind favor of going with me to help me settle my affairs?"

Since Dora was in good spirits and Aunt Betsey was with her, I agreed to go.

While I visited old friends in Yarmouth, Mr. Peggotty broke the news to Mrs. Peggotty and Ham. Soon the door of the boathouse stood open, with all of its furniture and goods ready to be shipped to the London docks. I took a last look at my old bedroom. Everything was gone, down to the little blue mug that had held the seaweed. I thought of myself, lying there, when that first great change was happening at my home when my mother married Mr. Murdstone. I thought of the days Emily and I had run along the beach. And I thought of Steerforth, and a foolish fear came over me—a fear that perhaps he was near and liable to turn around any corner.

David's Last Look at His Old Bedroom

Mr. Micawber Arrives at the Hotel.

CHAPTER 18

Uriah Heep's Downfall

When I returned from Yarmouth, the time for the mysterious appointment at Canterbury with Mr. Micawber had come.

When we reached the hotel, Mr. Micawber came to our rooms immediately.

"Now," said my aunt to Mr. Micawber, "we are ready for Mount Vesuvius or anything else."

"I believe you will witness an eruption shortly," said Mr. Micawber. "I will say only that I have been in communication with Mr. Traddles, and he has given me his best legal advice. Give me a start of five minutes and then come to the offices of Wickfield and Heep. There, ask for Agnes."

He bowed to us all and disappeared.

After five minutes, we followed him to the old house without saying one word on the way.

Mr. Micawber greeted us at the door with pretended surprise and showed us into the dining room. Hearing voices, Heep came in to investigate.

I had not seen Uriah Heep since I had struck him at Doctor Strong's. Our visit astonished him, and he frowned. Then, when Agnes entered, he quickly smiled.

"You may go, Micawber," said Heep. But seeing his clerk standing at the door, he shouted, "Did you not hear me tell you to go? Why are you waiting?"

"Because I *choose* to wait!"

Heep turned pale, then red with rage. "Oho! This is a conspiracy!" he cried, looking at the faces in the room.

"Oho! This Is a Conspiracy!"

Traddles began, in a calm, business-like voice, "I am the agent and friend of Mr. Wickfield. I have his written permission in my pocket to act as his attorney."

"The old idiot is drunk and out of his wits," cried Heep. "You got it from him by fraud."

"Something has been gotten from him by fraud, Heep," said Traddles, "and you know what that is."

Hatred raged in Heep's eyes as he glared at each of us in turn. Then Mr. Micawber stepped forward and took a document out of his pocket. It was a letter he had written, and as he read it, it proved to be an accusation of Heep's forgery of Mr. Wickfield's signature to take his money. As Heep's clerk, Micawber knew that Heep kept false books and charged Mr. Wickfield for bills that did not exist. We also learned that it was Heep who had stolen my aunt's money after she had invested it with Mr. Wickfield.

Heep made a dash at the letter as if to tear

Hatred Rages in Heep's Eyes.

it to pieces, but Mr. Micawber knocked Heep's hand away.

"You are to replace the money you stole, Heep," said Traddles, "and also cancel your partnership agreement with Mr. Wickfield."

"I won't do it!" cried Heep.

"Then perhaps the law will detain you," said Traddles. "Copperfield, get the police!"

"Stop!" growled Heep as I turned to go. "I'll give you everything."

"Good!" said Traddles. "Now go to your room and stay there until we have checked all the papers."

Now that Mr. Micawber had cleared his conscience, he returned to his family again as a happy man. He wanted to move to a new city to find work, and my aunt suggested that he go to Australia with Mr. Peggotty and Emily. She even offered to lend him the money for his passage. With his new prospects and peace of mind, Mr. Micawber was again a jovial man.

Traddles Orders Heep to His Room.

"I Have Been Very Happy with You."

CHAPTER 19

Death and Silence

Dora was ill for a long time. Did I know that my child-wife would leave me soon? The doctors told me, but I could not believe it.

One night she told me that perhaps it was better this way. "I was a young child," she said softly, "not in years, but in experience and thoughts. I was not fit to be a wife. I was not clever enough to understand the things that interested you."

I wept. "Oh, Dora, my love. I have been very happy with you, very, very happy. Do not speak that way."

Dora asked to see Agnes that night, and

while I sat by the fire, leaving my two loves to talk, Jip whined at my feet to go upstairs.

"Not tonight, Jip!" I said.

The dog lay down at my feet and stretched out . . . with a cry, he was dead!

At that moment, Agnes came down the stairs, her face full of pity and grief, her hands raised to Heaven. It was over. My dear Dora, my child-wife, was dead.

I came to think that my life was at an end, too, that my only refuge was the grave. But my aunt suggested that I travel abroad for a while. I agreed to go, but not until what Mr. Micawber called "the final pulverization of Heep" and not until the departure of the Micawbers and the Peggottys.

We returned to Canterbury—my aunt, Agnes and I—to find Traddles behind a heap of books and papers at a table in the Wickfield house. Traddles told us that Mr. Wickfield was in Mr. Dick's constant care and was much better and more like his old self.

Agnes Tells David That Dora is Dead.

After much paper work, Traddles determined that Mr. Wickfield would have enough money to keep his business and his property. This pleased Agnes.

"Next, Miss Trotwood," said Traddles, "I found that your money had not been invested and lost at all. Heep still had it. He didn't take it out of greed. He took it because he hated Copperfield and wanted to hurt him."

"He's a monster of meanness!" said my aunt.

And I thanked Heaven that Heep was gone away for good.

Immediately after Dora's death, my brokenhearted Peggotty left her brother with his last-minute travel preparations to spend some time with me. We talked of Ham, and I decided to go to Yarmouth to see him that very evening. Perhaps he'd want me to write a letter to Emily for him.

As I approached the little seaside town, the wind was blinding. Its gusts were filled with

Traddles Returns Aunt Betsey's Money.

flying stones and sand, and the rain came down like a shower of steel. The high watery rolls of the tremendous sea looked as if they would swallow the town. Still, crowds of people were running toward the beach.
"What is the matter?" I cried.

"A wreck! Close by! Make haste if you want to see her. She's a schooner from Spain. She'll go to pieces any minute!"

I ran to the beach, and there I saw the schooner, close in upon us!

One mast was broken off and entangled in a maze of sail and rigging. The ship was rolling violently. It was breaking up! At that moment, the sea swept over the rolling wreck, carrying men and planks and rails into the boiling surf.

No one on shore dared enter that raging sea to attempt a rescue. Then suddenly, I saw Ham breaking through the crowd toward the sea. I ran to him and tried to hold him back with both arms. But he was determined to go

David Tries To Hold Ham Back.

in to save the one man who was still clinging
to the mast—a man with long dark curls and
a bright red cap.

"Mas'r Davy," he said, grasping my two
hands, "if my time has come, 'tis come. If it
hasn't, I'll survive it. Lord above, bless you!"

A rope was tied around Ham's waist. He
ran into the sea, but was swept back by a
great wave. He was hurt; I saw blood on his
face. But he went in towards the wreck a second time. Just as he was within an arm's
reach, a high mountain of water sent the ship
to the bottom in a raging whirlpool! The men
on shore pulled on the rope and drew Ham
back to the beach at my feet. He was dead!

We carried him to the nearest house and as
I sat beside his lifeless body, a fisherman who
had known me when Emily and I were children came to the door.

"Sir," he said, with trembling lips, "will you
come back out with me?"

I suddenly thought of the sailor who had

Ham Is Dead.

held onto the mast before the ship went under. Terror-stricken, I asked the fisherman, "Has a body come ashore?"

"Yes."

"Do I know it?"

He didn't answer, but led me to the shore. And on that part of the beach where Emily and I as children had looked for shells, I saw him lying with his head upon his arm, as I had often seen him lying in his bed at school—James Steerforth!

They brought a hand-bier and laid him on it. All the men who carried him had known him, had gone sailing with him, and had seen him merry and bold.

I took his body to London that night and laid him in his mother's room. Mrs. Steerforth sat motionless, rigid, staring, moaning . . . but giving no other signs of life. I lifted his leaden hand and held it to my heart. All the world seemed filled with death and silence.

Steerforth's Body Is Washed Ashore.

Peggotty and David See Their Friends Off.

CHAPTER 20

My Return to Agnes

When Peggotty and I went to see our friends off, we were overjoyed to find that Mr. Peggotty was taking Martha along to Australia too. We said nothing of the two deaths, for we didn't want their happy departure spoiled.

I left England soon after, and for three years I traveled and wrote, sending my stories to Traddles to arrange for their publication. When my health had improved, I decided to return home.

Three years. Home had become very dear to me. Agnes had too. She had written to me during those three years, always cheerful and calming, telling me of the school she had opened for young girls. The more I thought of her during those three years, the more I realized how much I loved her and how good she was to me. I hoped it wasn't too late. I hoped she wasn't already married.

I landed in London on a wintry autumn night, and the next day, I was on the coach to Dover to see my aunt who had returned to her old seaside cottage. She and Mr. Dick and Peggotty welcomed me with tears of joy.

Late in the evening when we were alone, my aunt asked me, "And now, Trot, when are you going to see the Wickfields?"

"Tomorrow, I hope," I replied. "But is she ... is Agnes married?"

"She might have been married twenty times since you have been gone, but she didn't. Still, I suspect that there is someone who she will marry." And she smiled slyly.

"Then I'm sure she will tell me about him."

I rode away early the next morning. I was

Aunt Betsey Talks About Agnes.

overjoyed to see Agnes, but afraid of what she might tell me. We spoke of my trip and of the Peggottys. Then I asked, "And what of you, Agnes? What has happened in your life all this time?"

"Papa is well," she answered with a smile. "Our home is quiet and happy. That is all there is to tell."

"*All*, Agnes?" I asked. "Is there nothing else, dear sister?"

She shook her head, and a quiet smile appeared on her shining face.

"I want you to know, Agnes, that all my life I shall look up to you. I shall always love you as I do now and have always done. But you must talk now and tell me from your lips what I have heard from others—that there is someone you love, someone you will marry."

Agnes burst into tears and turned away from me. "If I have a secret, it must remain mine, as it has for years. I cannot reveal it."

"For years?" I cried, taking her in my arms

"I Shall Always Love You As I Do Now."

as a sudden realization hit me. Hopes whirled through my mind. "Dearest Agnes! Do I dare let myself believe . . . ?"

"My dear Trotwood, there is one thing I must say and never could bear to say—I have loved you all my life!"

Oh how happy we were! When we told my aunt, for the first time in my life I saw her cry hysterically—so hysterically that Peggotty and Mr. Dick came running into the parlor, whereupon my aunt gave them each a mighty hug.

Had my aunt deceived me about Agnes marrying someone else? I would never know.

Agnes and I were married within a fortnight. It was only afterwards that Agnes told me that on the night Dora died, she had sent for her for only one reason—she had asked Agnes, as her dying wish, to take her place as my wife.

And Agnes wept in telling me this. I wept too, though we were both so happy.

Miss Betsey Cries at the Happy News.

Happily Married for Ten Years

CHAPTER 21

A Visitor from Australia

I became famous and wealthy as a writer, and my life with Agnes was a joy.

We had been married ten happy years. Agnes and I were sitting by the fire in our house in London, and three of our children were playing in the room when a servant entered and told me that a stranger wished to see me.

"Has he come on business?" I asked.

"No," answered the servant, "he is an old man. He looks like a farmer." This sounded mysterious to the children.

"Let him come in," I said.

DAVID COPPERFIELD

A healthy-looking, gray-haired old man stood in the doorway.

"It is Mr. Peggotty!" cried Agnes as she ran to embrace him.

When our joyous greetings were over, we sat before the fire, he with our children on his knees.

"I'm not growing younger," he said, "and it was always on my mind these thirteen years that I must come and see Mas'r Davy afore I got to be too old."

"And now tell us," I said, "tell us everything about our friends back in Australia."

"We worked hard at first," he said, "but we are thriving with our sheep farm."

"And Emily?" Agnes and I asked together.

"She didn't learn of Ham's death for nearly a year when I did, from an Englishman traveling through our town. She was depressed for a while, but she kept busy with her farm work. She's had many opportunities to marry, but as she says, 'Uncle, that's gone

Mr. Peggotty on a Visit from Australia

forever.' She spends her time teaching children and tending to the sick and to her loving uncle."

"And Martha?" I asked.

"Married to a fine young man—a farmer."

"Now, last, but not least, Mr. Micawber?" I asked.

"Worked at farming for several years, but now the gentleman's a Magistrate in our town and much respected and loved by all."

Mr. Peggotty stayed with us for a month, and before he returned to Australia, he asked me to go with him to Yarmouth to visit Ham's grave. While I was copying the plain inscription from the tablet, at his request, I saw him stoop and gather up a tuft of grass from the grave.

"For Emily," he said as he put the grass in his pocket. "I promised her, Mas'r Davy."

A Tuft of Grass for Emily

Godmother to a Real Betsey Trotwood

CHAPTER 22

Happiness!

And now my written story ends. Here is my aunt, wearing spectacles, well over eighty years old, yet who still walks six miles at a stretch in winter weather. She is godmother to a real living Betsey Trotwood, my daughter, and she is happy.

Always with her, here comes Peggotty, her cheeks and arms shriveled, but her rough finger ready to scold my children as it once did me. There is something bulky in Peggotty's arms. It is the crocodile book, in a rather dilapidated condition by this time.

And now my children read to her of the "crorkindills."

Among my boys, this summer holiday time, I see an old man making giant kites and gazing at them in the air with delight. Now and then Mr. Dick stops me to tell me that my aunt is the most wonderful of women.

The Doctor, always our good friend, still works at his Dictionary, and is somewhere about the letter D.

My lamp burns low, and I have written far into the night. The shining face of my beautiful Agnes is beside me as I work; our children sleep soundly above us. I hope to know this happiness for many years.

An Old Man Still Makes Giant Kites.